LAKELIFE

LAKELIFE

Willow Creek Press®

Published by Willow Creek Press, Inc.
P.O. Box 147, Minocqua, Wisconsin 54548

Photographs © the following contributors

p10 © DenisTangneyJr/istockphoto.com; p11 © Martin Wahlborg/istockphoto.com; p12 © Sundbird/istockphoto.com; p17 © Jirawat Cheepsumol/500px.com; p22 top right © Arthur Matkovskyy/istockphoto.com; bottom right © acincin/istockphoto.com; p23 © Erdjan Bekir/500px.com; p30 © TeuvoSalmenjoki/istockphoto.com; p33 © LawrenceSawyer/istockphoto.com; p34 © Dashabelozerova/istockphoto.com; p44 © Paul Frederiksen/500px.com; p47 © Mampfred/istockphoto.com; p48 © Kyle Meck/500px.com; p52 © Rick Parchen/ParchenPhotography/500px.com; p58 © Dario Bosi/500px.com; p64 © titoslack/istockphoto.com; p70 © wingmar/istockphoto.com; p71 © ShootnBang/istockphoto.com; p76 © Rob Taylor/500px.com; p78 © GeorgePeters/istockphoto.com; p79 © sikeshouse/500px.com; p80 © adamschmisek/istockphoto.com; p82 © dwservingHim/istockphoto.com; p84 © GomezDavid/istockphoto.com; p85 © GomezDavid/istockphoto.com; p86 © beebul/istockphoto.com; p94 © OGphoto/istockphoto.com; p99 © pomarinus/istockphoto.com; p102 © Oliver/500px.com; p110 © Adventure Joe/500px.com; p111 © allgord/istockphoto.com; p113 © ImagineGolf/istockphoto.com; p129 © Springfrom/istockphoto.com; p134 © Michal Boubin/istockphoto.com; p136 © DenisTangneyJr/istockphoto.com; p140 © shaunl/istockphoto.com; p141 © Andrey Danilovich/istockphoto.com; p142 © jordachelr/istockphoto.com;

Printed in China

Table of Contents

(LAK) n. 1. A large inland body of fresh water.
2. A scenic pond.
—*Webster's*

THE LAKE

Lakes large and small with countless names abound throughout North America, but the odds are you are drawn to one in particular. To you and your family and friends, your special body of water is simply referred to as "the lake." And any time you are away you can't wait to rest your eyes upon its bright and shimmering surface. Close your eyes. You see it now, don't you?

IT'S PEACEFUL DOWN BY THE WATER NOT MUCH TO DO OR SEE, BUT EVERYTHING TO HEAR AND FEEL.

M<small>Y</small> CONNECTION TO THE
EARTH IS REINFORCED
THROUGH THE RHYTHM
OF THE WAVES.

—*Mike Dolan*

It is in the still silence of nature
where one will find true bliss.

—J.J.C.

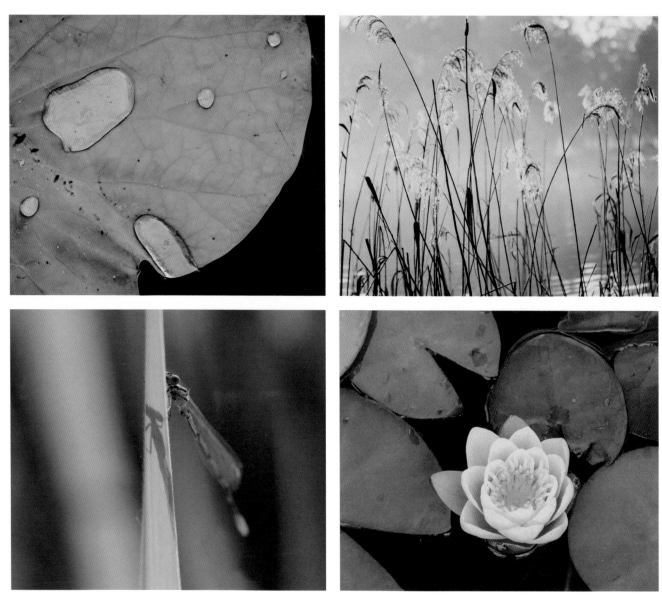

A LAKE IS THE LANDSCAPE'S MOST
BEAUTIFUL AND EXPRESSIVE FEATURE.
IT IS EARTH'S EYE; LOOKING INTO
WHICH THE BEHOLDER MEASURES
THE DEPTH OF HIS OWN NATURE.

—Henry David Thoreau

A DAY AT THE LAKE RESTORES THE SOUL.

What is the good of having a nice house
without a decent planet to put it on?
—*Henry David Thoreau*

SHELTER

As lakes come in all shapes and sizes, so do the shelters that we erect along their lovely shores. They range from majestic chateaus to sprawling trophy homes, simple family cottages that go back generations, weekly rental cabins, and humble tents. Regardless of the structure, all of them have two things in common: (1) a roof overhead, elaborate or simple and, most importantly, (2) a sweeping lake view.

YOUR DEEPEST ROOTS ARE IN NATURE. NO MATTER
WHO YOU ARE, WHERE YOU LIVE, OR WHAT KIND
OF LIFE YOU LEAD, YOU REMAIN IRREVOCABLY
LINKED WITH THE REST OF CREATION.

—*Charles Cook*

THE HUMAN SPIRIT NEEDS
PLACES WHERE NATURE HAS
NOT BEEN REARRANGED BY
THE HAND OF MAN.

THERE IS NOTHING LIKE RETURNING TO A PLACE
THAT REMAINS UNCHANGED TO FIND THE WAYS IN
WHICH YOU YOURSELF HAVE ALTERED.

—*Nelson Mandela*

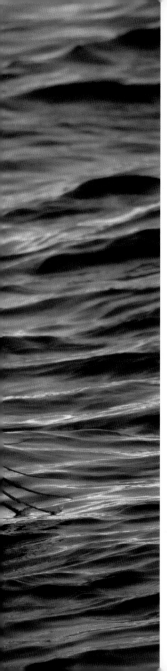

In all things nature there is something of the marvelous.
—*Aristotle*

LAKESIDE NEIGHBORS

We view our wild neighbors with awe and wonder when they appear along the shoreline, upon the lake's surface, and flying overhead. Their presence among us enriches our lives, lifts our souls, and multiplies the already many pleasures of lake living.

But there are also other neighbors, unwelcome, bothersome ones at that, secretly dwelling within our walls, under the eaves, inside the garbage, and humming in the summer air. Some of these critters are cringeworthy, most are merely annoying, and together they comprise an inevitable, inconvenient fact of lake living with which we simply learn to abide.

ANIMALS ARE SUCH AGREEABLE
FRIENDS. THEY ASK NO QUESTIONS,
THEY PASS NO CRITICISMS.

—*George Eliot*

STUDY NATURE, LOVE NATURE, STAY CLOSE
TO NATURE. IT WILL NEVER FAIL YOU.
—*Frank Lloyd Wright*

EACH SPECIES IS A MASTERPIECE, A CREATION
ASSEMBLED WITH EXTREME CARE AND GENIUS.
—*Edward O. Wilson*

If only it could be like this always—
always summer, the fruit always ripe.
—*Evelyn Waugh*

LAKESIDE LIVING

Arise to the morning songs of birds and wavelets calmly lapping on the shoreline. Soon comes the rapid thump-thump-thump of bare feet running on the dock followed by splashing water and shrieks of laughter. Thus begins a day filled with the simple joys and activities of lake living where everyone, even the family dog, is bound together in pure happiness.

You're outside the tension zone now. Think sun, fun, flip-flops, wet swimming suits, and damp bath towels later yielding to campfires, starlight serenity, s'mores and, on a good night, lightning bugs.

A VACATION IS HAVING NOTHING TO
DO AND ALL DAY TO DO IT IN.
—*Robert Orben*

SUMMER IS THE TIME WHEN ONE
SHEDS ONE'S TENSIONS WITH
ONE'S CLOTHES, AND THE RIGHT
KIND OF DAY IS JEWELED BALM
FOR THE BATTERED SPIRIT...

—*Ada Louise Huxtable*

SUMMER AFTERNOON—TO ME THOSE HAVE ALWAYS BEEN THE TWO MOST BEAUTIFUL WORDS IN THE ENGLISH LANGUAGE.

—Henry James

REST IS NOT IDLENESS, AND TO LIE
SOMETIMES ON THE GRASS UNDER
THE TREES ON A SUMMER'S DAY,
LISTENING TO THE MURMUR OF
WATER, OR WATCHING THE CLOUDS
FLOAT ACROSS THE SKY, IS BY
NO MEANS A WASTE OF TIME.

—John Lubbock

MANY GO FISHING ALL THEIR LIVES WITHOUT KNOWING
THAT IT IS NOT FISH THEY ARE AFTER.

—*Henry David Thoreau*

THE CHARM OF FISHING IS THAT
IT IS THE PURSUIT OF WHAT IS
ELUSIVE BUT ATTAINABLE,
A PERPETUAL SERIES OF
OCCASIONS FOR HOPE.

—*John Buchan*

LAND WAS CREATED TO PROVIDE
A PLACE FOR BOATS TO VISIT.
—*Brooks Atkinson*

IF BREAD IS THE FIRST NECESSITY OF LIFE,
RECREATION IS A CLOSE SECOND.

—*Edward Bellamy*

THE FIRST TIME WHEN A SAIL TRULY
FILLED AND THE BOAT TOOK LIFE AND
KNIFED ACROSS THE LAKE UNDER
PERFECT CONTROL, THIS WAS SO
BEAUTIFUL IT STOPPED MY BREATH.

—*Gary Paulsen*

TODAY'S LAKE FORECAST: ABUNDANT SUNSHINE, VARIABLE WINDS WITH A CHANCE OF COCKTAILS.

P<small>ART OF THE SECRET OF</small>
S<small>UCCESS IN LIFE IS TO EAT</small>
<small>WHAT YOU LIKE AND LET</small>
<small>THE FOOD FIGHT IT OUT</small>
<small>ON THE INSIDE.</small>

—*Mark Twain*

THERE IS NO SINCERER LOVE
THAN THE LOVE OF FOOD.
—*George Bernard Shaw*

WHAT GREATER BLESSING TO
GIVE THANKS FOR AT A FAMILY
GATHERING THAN THE FAMILY
AND THE GATHERING.

—Robert Brault

THE BEST THING ONE CAN DO WHEN IT'S RAINING IS TO LET IT RAIN.

—*Henry Wadsworth Longfellow*

RAINBOWS APOLOGIZE FOR ANGRY SKIES.

—Sylvia Voirol

There is something deep within us that sobs at endings.
Why, God, does everything have to end? Why does all nature
grow old? Why do spring and summer have to go?
—Joe Wheeler

SEASON'S END

Knowing that it would come to an end does not make it any easier to accept. But now it's time to pack the car, close the lake house, and take one last walk down the dock. Stand there and hold this last image of your beloved lake in your mind—you'll want to refer back to it often upon your return to the workaday world. Close your eyes. You see it now, don't you?

IN THE DEPTH OF WINTER, I FINALLY LEARNED THAT
WITHIN ME THERE LAY AN INVINCIBLE SUMMER.

—*Albert Camus*

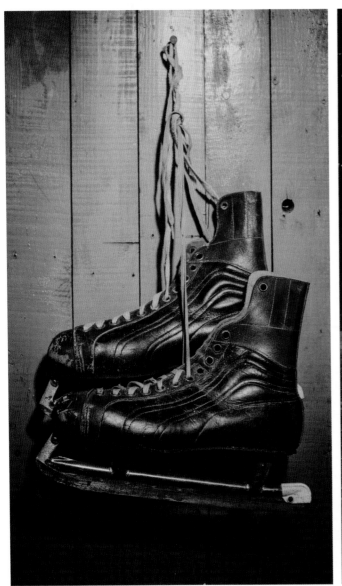